Graph Algorithms

for the day before your Coding Interview

Aditya Chatterjee x Ue Kiao

Introduction

Graph Algorithms are fundamentally important and different than other Algorithmic domains as it gives an inherent structure to the data and we operate on it. This is one of the most important domains for Coding Interviews focused on problem solving.

Following are some of the problems we have explored which involve ideas to solve a wider range of problems:

- **All paths between two vertices**

This is a fundamental problem as modifications to it results in solving a wide range of problems.

In the process of formulating a solution, we have explored core ideas like graph traversal techniques like Depth First Search and Graph representation like Adjacency List.

- **Mother Vertex**

This is an important problem as it highlights two key ideas of Graph problems that is connectivity and importance of specific vertices.

We have solved this problem using two approaches where the efficient approach is a modification of Depth First Search and takes $O(V^2)$ time complexity.

- **Paths with K edges**

This is an important problem as it demonstrates how we can utilize ideas from Dynamic Programming and Divide and Conquer to solve Graph Problems.

We have demonstrated four approaches where the brute force approach takes $O(2^V \times V)$ time, improving it with a structure we get to $O(V^K)$ time, further applying Dynamic Programming to it, we get to $O(V^3 * K)$ time and finally, using Divide and Conquer to optimize calculation, we arrive at $O(V^3 * \log K)$ time.

This is a perfect Graph Algorithm problem.

We have covered more variants of the problems and ideas in our conclusion to give a bigger picture and better equip you to solve any problem.

Let us get started with our problems.

Problem 1: All paths between two vertices

This is a fundamental problem as traversing is the most basic operation on the graph and modifications to it results in solving a wide range of problems.

In the process to solve this problem, we get the fundamental concepts such as **Adjacency List** and **Depth First Search** as well and see how the ideas can be used to solve other problems.

Our problem is given a graph, we need to **find all paths between two vertices**.

Formally, our problem is: Given a directed graph, a vertex 'v1' and a vertex 'v2', print all paths from given 'v1' to 'v2'.

Consider the following directed graph as an example. Let the v1 be 0 and v2 be 6. There are 4 different paths from 0 to 6.

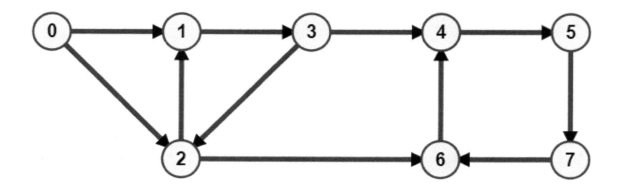

Below are the paths between 0 and 6:

- 0->1->3->2->6
- 0->1->3->4->5->7->6
- 0->2->1->3->4->5->7->6
- 0->2->6

How to find path between two vertices?

- **Case 1: Undirected Connected Graph**: In this case, there is always a path between given two vertices as the graph is connected and each edge is bi-directional (means we can move in any direction).

- **Case 2: Undirected/ Directed Disconnected Graph**: In this case, there is no path between vertices across disconnected groups.

- **Case 3: Directed Connected Graph**: In this case, we must check whether path exist between the given two vertices or not.

The idea to find if there is a path between two vertices is to do **Depth First Traversal** of given directed graph. We can use **Breadth First Search** as well which we will discuss further later.

Let us review the pseudocode of Depth First Search:

```
depth-first-search(graph G, vertex V)
```

```
{
        // Can be done using an array
        Mark vertex V as visited

        // Go deeper
        For all vertices X connected to V directly with an
edge:
                if X is not visited:
                        depth-first-search(G, X)

}
```

The above is a recursive approach. We can implement it iteratively as well:

```
depth-first-search(graph G, vertex V)
{
        Let S be a stack
        Push vertex V into S
        while S is not empty
                X = pop element from S
                If X is not visited
                        Mark X as visited
                        for all edges from X to Y in G
                                Push Y into S
}
```

The only difference in Breadth First Search is that we process all vertices at the same level first and then, move to the next level. In DFS, we move to deeper levels as opportunity comes.

Let us return to our sub-problem: "**Find if there is a path between two vertices**".

The simple solution is to apply BFS or DFS from the starting vertex V1 and see if we reach vertex V2.

The steps are as follows:

- Start the traversal from 'v1'.
- Keep storing the visited vertices in an array or list say 'path[]'.
- If we reach the vertex 'v2', pathExist (a Boolean variable) becomes true and print contents of path[].

The important thing is to mark current vertices in path[] as visited also, so that the traversal does not go in a cycle. If there is no path between the vertices, then pathExist remains false.

Now, we must extend this basic approach to find all paths.

Think carefully about what algorithmic change is required.

The basic idea is to somehow backtrack once a path is found so that another path is found.

Approach: Use modified Depth First Search

- Mark all the nodes as not visited and create and empty path (to store temporary paths).

- Start from the vertex v1 and visit the next vertex (use adjacency list).

- Keep track of visited nodes to avoid cycles.

- Add current vertex to result to keep track of path from vertex v1.

Now if you **observe carefully**, the new problem is to find all paths from the current vertex to destination. For instance, as per the example above, start from vertex 0 and visit vertex 1. Now all the paths from vertex 1 to vertex 5 will be included in our result if we add vertex 0. So, make a recursive call with source as vertex 1 and destination as vertex 5.

- Once we reach the destination vertex, print the path.

- The next step is to mark the current node as not visited and remove it from path.

- Now visit the next node in adjacency list in step 1 and repeat all the steps (loop)

Pseudocode:

```
// Find all paths
all-paths(vertex V1, vertex V2, graph G, path P)
// Path P is empty initially
{
    Mark vertex V1 as visited
    Add V1 to path P // Extra step

    // Extra if else condition
    if( V1 == V2)
    {
        print path P
    }
    else
    {
        for all edges from V1 to X in G
            if X is not visited
                all-paths(X, V2)
    }

    Mark V1 as not visited
    Remove V1 from path P
}
```

Example:

all-paths() simply performs the DFS from the given vertex V1 and traverses through vertices which are reachable from given vertex.

To understand this deeply, we will apply this on our original graph and demonstrate each step. Following is our graph:

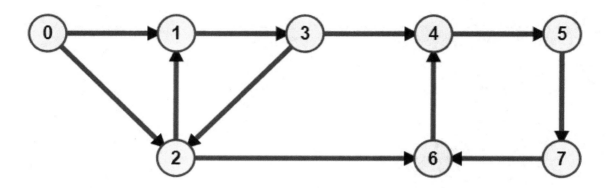

Let us take an example all the paths from 0 to 6.

Below is the adjacency list of all the vertex for reference

Adjacency List		
0:	1	2
1:	3	
2:	1	6
3:	2	4
4:	5	
5:	7	
6:	4	
7:	6	

Start the DFS from vertex 0 mark the current vertex 0 as visited and add it to path[] array so path[] array contains one element 0 and increase the path index.

We will check if the current vertex 0 is the destination vertex 6. It is not so we go into the adjacency list (which contains information about the connections of current vertex) of vertex 0 we which contains 1 and 2.

Check vertex 1 is visited and go the vertex 1.

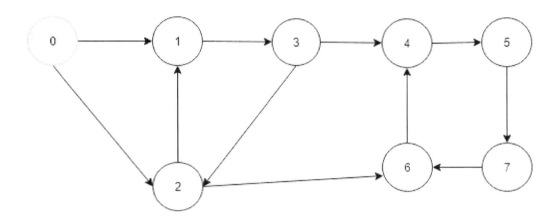

Now it is new problem of **finding all paths from 1 to 6** so we call the function again.

Now current vertex is 1 so it is marked as visited. Store the current vertex 1 into path[] so it contains two elements 0 and 1, increase the path index and check if it is the destination vertex 6. If it not the destination vertex, so go to adjacency list of vertex 1 which contains 3.

Check vertex 3 is visited and now go to the vertex 3.

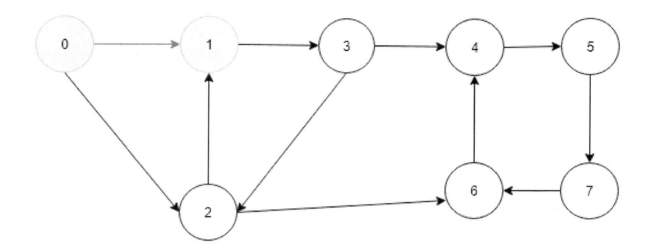

The new problem is: **finding all paths from 3 to 6**.

Now, current vertex is 3 and same as above, we mark it as visited. There are three 3 visited vertices 0, 1 and 3 and add to the path[] so now it contains three elements 0, 1 and 3.

Check if it is destination vertex. As it is not, go to the adjacency list of vertex 3 which contains 2 and 4. Check vertex 2 as visited and go to vertex 2.

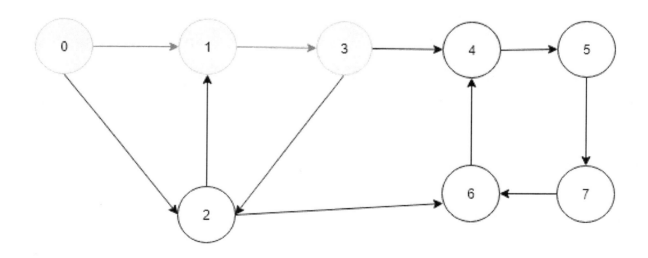

Now, the sub-problem is: **finding path from 2 to 6**.

Now the current vertex is 2 so we mark it as visited. There are 4 elements marked as visited 0, 1, 3 and 2 and add it to the path[] so now it contains four elements 0, 1, 3 and 2.

Check if is destination vertex and as it is not, go to the adjacency list of vertex 2 which contains 1 and 6.

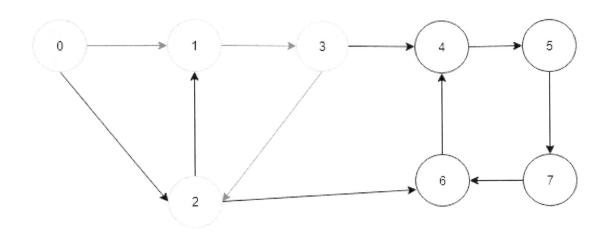

As vertex 1 is marked as visited, we move to vertex 6.

The current vertex is 6 so we mark it as visited and add to the path[] so it is contains 0, 1, 3, 2 and 6.

Check the current vertex 6 is the destination vertex. It is same so we make the pathExist true and print path[].

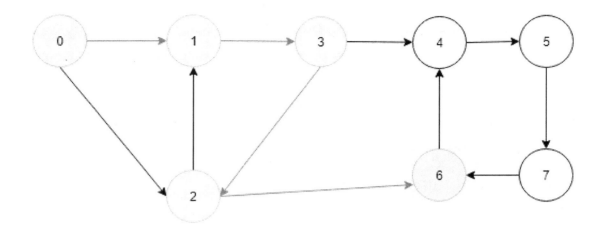

Path printed: **0 -> 1 -> 3 -> 2 -> 6**

There can be one then more path exist between two nodes, so we must backtrack. We mark the current vertex 6 as not visited and delete it from path[] and return to the step where it is called.

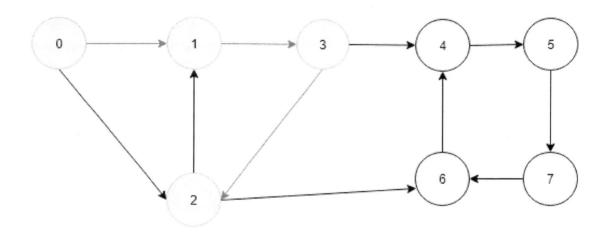

Now there is no more elements into the adjacency list of vertex 2 and same as above, we mark the vertex 2 as not visited and delete it from path[].

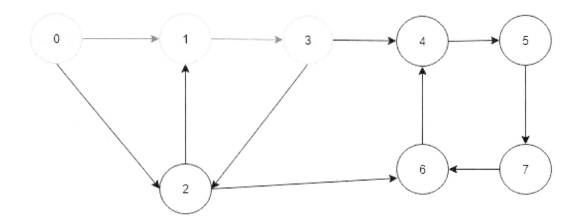

Now again, we return to the vertex 3 and another element of adjacency list of vertex 3 that is vertex 4 is not visited so we go to the vertex 4.

The problem at this point is: **finding all paths between vertex 4 and 6.**

We mark our current vertex 4 as visited and add to the path[] now it contains four elements 0, 1, 3, and 4.

Check if it is destination vertex and as it is not, we go to adjacency list of current vertex 4 which contains 5.

Check if vertex 5 is visited and as it is not, we go to the vertex 5 and recall the function again to **find all paths between 5 and 6.**

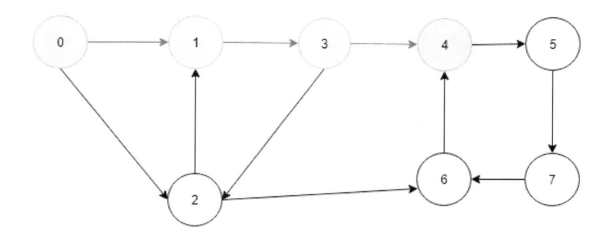

We mark our current vertex 5 as visited and add to the path[] now it contains 0, 1, 3, 4 and 5.

Check if current vertex 5 is destination vertex and as it is not, we go to adjacency list of vertex 5 which contains 7. We check if vertex 7 is visited and as it not, we go to vertex 7 and recall the function to **find all paths between 7 and 6**.

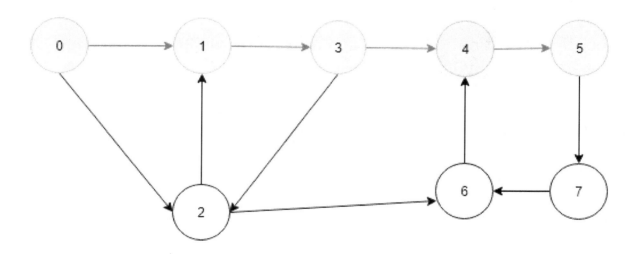

We mark our current vertex 7 as visited and add to the path[] now it contains 0, 1, 3, 4, 5 and 7.

We check if current vertex 7 is destination vertex and as it is not, we go to adjacency list of vertex 7 which contains 6.

Check vertex 6 is visited and as it is not, we go to vertex 6 and recall the function to **find the path between 6 and 6**.

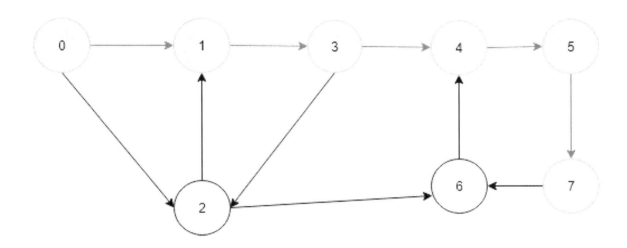

We mark our current vertex 6 as visited and add to the path[] which contains 0, 1, 3, 4, 5, 7 and 6.

We check if current vertex 6 is destination vertex and it is so, we print the path and mark vertex 6 as not visited and delete it from path once again as explain above.

Path: **0 -> 1 -> 3 -> 4 -> 5 -> 7 -> 6**

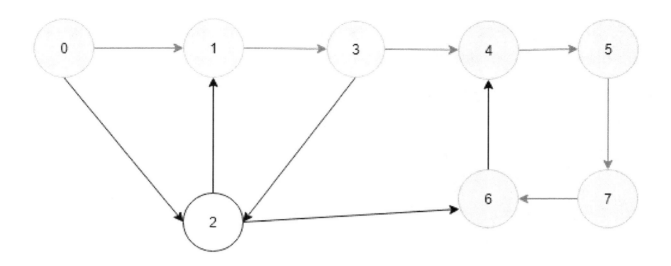

Do same thing again (backtrack) and get the last two paths.

Complexity Analysis

The key points to note are that if a graph has V vertices:

- There can be **O(V²) edges** (E) which is called a dense graph
- The maximum length of a path between two nodes will be **O(V)** without loops
- There can be **O(2^V) paths** between two nodes as for a potential path, a vertex can be a part of it or not (2 options) and there are V such potential vertices.

Time Complexity of our approach: **O(2^V x (V+E))**

We can have exponentially many paths, and for each such path, our prepending operation will be **O(V+E)**. If we want to check the path

---

between two nodes exist or not then, it can be checked in in one DFS **O(V+E)**.

Space Complexity of our approach: $\mathbf{O(2^V \times V)}$

This is because that are 2^V paths and each path can have at most V vertices.

This is an important problem as this can be considered as the first approach to solve a wide range of problems such as:

- Find k^{th} longest path between two nodes
- Number of paths with K edges between two nodes
- Shortest path between two nodes
- Longest path between two nodes

and much more fundamental problems.

With this problem, we have a strong fundamental idea.

Let us move to our next problem.

Problem 2: Mother Vertex

This is an important problem as it highlights two key ideas of Graph problems:

- Connectivity is a central idea
- Importance to specific vertices

One such important type of vertex is known as **Mother Vertex**.

A mother vertex in a graph is a vertex from which we can reach all the nodes in the graph through directed path. In other words, A mother vertex in a graph $G = (V, E)$ is a vertex v such that all other vertices in G can be reached by a path from v.

Our problem is to **find the Mother Vertex in a given Graph**.

We have demonstrated two approaches:

- Brute Force approach **$O(V^3)$ time**
- Improved approach using modified Depth First Search **$O(V^2)$ time**

Example:

Consider the following Graph:

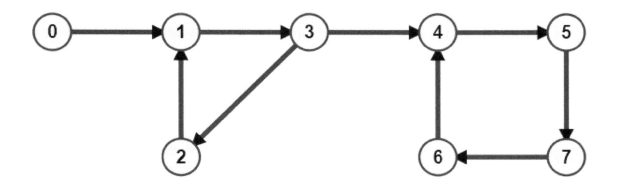

Vertices reachable from vertex 0:

0 -> 1 -> 3 -> 2 -> 4 -> 5 -> 7 -> 6

Vertices reachable from vertex 1:

1 -> 3 -> 2 -> 4 -> 5 -> 7 -> 6

Vertices reachable from vertex 2:

2 -> 1 -> 3 -> 4 -> 5 -> 7 -> 6

Vertices reachable from vertex 3:

3 -> 2 -> 1 -> 4 -> 5 -> 7 -> 6

Vertices reachable from vertex 4:

4 -> 5 -> 7 -> 6

Vertices reachable from vertex 5:

5 -> 7 -> 6 -> 4

Vertices reachable from vertex 6:

6 -> 4 -> 5 -> 7

Vertices reachable from vertex 7:

7 -> 6 -> 4 -> 5

The vertex from which all other vertices are reachable is **vertex 0**

There can be more than one mother vertices in a graph. We need to output anyone of them. For Example, in the below graph, vertices 0, 1 and 2 are mother vertices.

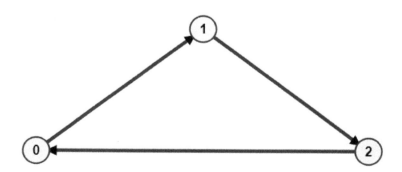

How to find mother vertex?

- **Case 1: Undirected Connected Graph**: In this case, all the vertices are mother vertices as we can reach to all the other nodes in the graph.

- **Case 2: Undirected/Directed Disconnected Graph**: In this case, there is no mother vertex as we cannot reach to all the other nodes in the graph from a vertex.

- **Case 3: Directed Connected Graph**: In this case, we have to find a vertex **v** in the graph such that we can reach to all the other vertices in the graph through a directed path.

A simple approach

A trivial approach will be to perform Depth First Search (DFS) or Breadth First Search (BFS) on all the vertices and find whether we can reach all the nodes in the graph.

The steps are as follows:

- For every vertex v in graph G
    - Do DFS or BFS from vertex v and mark each vertex as visited
    - If all vertices have been marked as visited
        - V is a mother vertex
- If no such vertex has been found, there is no mother vertex.

The pseudocode is as follows:

```
mother-vertex = -1

for every vertex V in graph G
    Mark all vertices as not visited
    Run Depth First Search from vertex V

    // Check if all vertices have been visited
    visited = true
    for every vertex X in graph G
        if X is not visited
            visited = false

    if visited = true
        mother-vertex = V
        End of program
```

The time complexity for this approach is **O(V x (V+E))** as:

- There are V vertices
- DFS or BFS takes O(V+E) time for each vertex

If the graph is a dense graph, then the number of edges (E) will be of the order of **O(V²)** which will bring the time complexity of our approach to **O(V³)**.

With an insight into the structure of the graph, we can solve this problem efficiently.

Better approach

The mother vertex can be found in **O(V+E)** time complexity. In a graph of strongly connected components, mother vertices are always vertices of source component in component graph. The idea is based on below fact (*We have explained all terms further in the explanation*).

If there exist mother vertex (or vertices), then one of the mother vertices is the last finished vertex in DFS (or a mother vertex has the maximum finish time in DFS traversal)

A vertex is said to be finished in DFS if a recursive call for its DFS is over, i.e., all descendants of the vertex have been visited.

We will understand this statement with a proof and intuitively as well.

Let us understand the fact intuitively.

Depth First Search is a simple traversal of the entire graph. The basic property is that it goes to the deepest vertex first that is it gives priority to depth rather than vertices at the same level (done by Breadth First Search).

A **strongly connected component** is a set of vertices such that from any vertex, we can reach any other vertex in the component. Every vertex is a mother vertex in this case for that component.

A graph may have several such strongly connected components.

If there is no edge between any particular strongly connected component, then there will be no mother vertex as a particular set of vertices will remain unreachable.

If there are edges between every strongly connected component, then we can reach vertices across components. We need to find the vertex which is the mother vertex considering all components.

Let us say that vertex A is the mother vertex and vertex B is not the mother vertex, but we assume it is be so.

If we run DFS from B, we cannot reach all vertices as it is not a mother vertex. In this case, we need to check which vertices have not been visited and we need to run DFS from it.

If there is an edge from B to A, then we will reach all vertices as A is a mother vertex. In this case, B will be a mother vertex as well.

We need to check if the last processed vertex is a mother vertex or not. This is because we need to consider the case of disconnected graphs.

If we run DFS from a mother vertex, then all vertices will be reached.

It may seem that we can **running DFS multiple times** but note that each vertex is being processed only once, hence the time complexity will remain the same as in the case of a single DFS.

Let us go through the **algorithm** and **pseudocode** first to understand it better.

Algorithm:

- Do the DFS traversal of the give graph and keep the track of last finished vertex 'v'.
- Then check if v is the mother vertex of the given graph by doing DFS.
- If v is not the mother vertex, then mother vertex does not exist for the given graph.

The steps are as follows:

- All vertices are marked "not visited"
- For every vertex v in graph G

- o If vertex v is not visited
    - ▪ Run Depth First Search (DFS) from vertex v and mark all reached vertices as visited
    - ▪ Let mother vertex be v
- Check if the last assumed mother vertex reaches all vertices by running DFS from it
- If above test is true, the last assumed mother vertex is our answer or else there is no mother vertex in the graph

Pseudocode:

```
mother-vertex = -1
Mark all vertices as not visited

for every vertex V in graph G

    If vertex V is not visited
        Run Depth First Search from vertex V
        mother-vertex = V

// Check if Mother Vertex reaches all vertices
Mark all vertices as not visited
Run Depth First Search from vertex mother-vertex

for every vertex V in graph G
    if vertex V is not visited
        mother-vertex = -1
        // Mother vertex does not exist
```

Let us move back to our original fact and see why it is true by a proof.

Let the last finished vertex be v. Basically, we need to prove that there cannot be an edge from another vertex u to v if u is not another mother vertex (Or there cannot exist a non-mother vertex u such that u → v is an edge).

There can be two possibilities:

- Recursive DFS call is made for u before v
- Recursive DFS call is made for v before u

Recursive DFS call is made for u before v. If an edge u → v exists, then v must have finished before u because v is reachable through u and a vertex finishes after all its descendants.

Recursive DFS call is made for v before u. In this case also, if an edge u → v exists, then either v must finish before u (which contradicts our assumption that v is finished at the end) OR u should be reachable from v (which means u is another mother vertex).

Hence, with this, we have proved our central fact based on which our efficient algorithm operates.

The time Complexity of our efficient approach is **O(V+E)** as:

- Depth First Search (DFS) takes O(V+E) time
- DFS is performed multiple times but each vertex is processed once as we maintain a single visited vertices record

---

Think of this carefully and analyze if Breath First Search can be used for this problem.

The simple answer is BFS can be used as well as connectivity is the central idea of the problem. There are specific problems which can be solved only through DFS or BFS. Think of these problems.

Focus on the key ideas we presented at the beginning of this problem.

Problem 3: K edge Path

This is an important problem as we bring in ideas from Dynamic Programming to solve a challenging and insightful Graph Problem.

- It shows how native approaches like Dynamic Programming can be applied to a graph problem
- It presents a case where a divide and conquer approach is faster than a Dynamic Programming approach
- It illustrates key ideas which can be used to solve one of the toughest graph problems

The problem is that given a graph, we need to find the number of paths from a vertex (say u) to another vertex (say v) with exactly K edges. Let us define that the graph has V vertices and E edges.

Pause and think for a couple of minutes before proceeding further.

This might seem to be a simple problem but solving this efficiently will require great insights. We will solve this step by step and go through three approaches:

- Brute force $O(2^V \times V)$ time
- Structured Brute force $O(V^K)$ time
- Dynamic Programming $O(V^3 * K)$ time
- Divide and Conquer $O(V^3 * \log K)$ time

Brute Force Approach

The key idea is to utilize the ideas we gained in our first problem where we found all paths between two vertices.

We need to find all paths between the two vertices and keep a count of the paths that have K edges in them.

The steps are:

- For all paths P from vertex V to U
  - If path P has K edges, then include P as a part of our answer

The time complexity from this problem is same as our first problem as the extra step can be implemented as an integral part of the algorithm. The time complexity will be $O(2^V \times V)$.

This is an exponential solution and we need to improve it further.

One idea to explore is that paths will K-1 edges to vertices directly connected to either V or U will be part of our answer potentially.

Structured Brute Force

This is a simple approach as we just need to traverse the graph and keep track of the edges encountered. A simple way is to implement it recursively. The key idea is to utilize answers of sub-problems (say K-1 edges path).

We call it a **structured Brute Force** as we use the results of K-1 edge paths to get the answers to K edge paths.

The recursive structure will be as:

paths (adjacency_matrix, source_vertex, destination_vertex, edges_permitted)

We start with the source vertex as u and then, move to all adjacent vertices of u and make a recursive call on that vertex as the source vertex. In this case, the edges permitted is decremented by 1 as we have already traversed an edge.

We add up all recursive calls which successfully reach the destination vertex using all the edges as permitted. If is simple to manage as if destination vertex is reach and edges permitted goes to 0, we have found a path and we return 1. In other cases, we shall return 0. We will add up all such return values and get our answer.

The pseudocode is as follows:

```
int numberOfPathsNaive(adjacency_list adj, int u, int v, int k)
{
    int __v = adj.size();
    if(k == 0 and u == v)
        return 1;
    if(k == 1 and adj[u][v])
        return 1;
    if(k <= 0)
        return 0;
    int res = 0;
    for(int i = 0; i < __v; ++ i)
    {
        if(adj[u][i])
        {
            res += numberOfPathsNaive(adj, i, v, k - 1);
        }
    }
    return res;
}
```

As we are traversing the entire graph with all possible edges, the time complexity of our brute force approach is **exponential** that is $O(V^K)$ where V is the number of vertices and K is the number of edges.

As a path can have at most K edges (without loops) and each edge can have any of the V vertices as pairs, the total number of possible paths becomes **$O(V^K)$** from which we need to find the number of paths that is within our focus.

As our brute force approach takes exponential time, it is not practical to use it for graphs beyond a certain size. We need to find an optimal approach.

Dynamic Programming Approach

We will take up a **Dynamic Programming approach** to solve this problem which will give a major boost.

In dynamic programing approach we use a 3D matrix table to store the number of paths:

---

dp[i][j][e] stores the number of paths from i to j with exactly e edges.

We fill the table in bottom up manner, we start from e=0 and fill the table till e=k. Then we have our answer stored in **dp[u][v][k]** where u is source, v is destination and k is number edges between path from source to destination.

```
dp[u][v][k] = number of paths from u to v with k edges
```

The idea of the relation is if there is an edge between vertex i and b, then dp[i][j][e] += dp[b][j][e-1] as one edge has been covered while going from vertex i to b.

The number of paths from vertex b to j is included in the set of paths from vertex i to j because there is an edge from vertex i to b.

Following code snippet covers the idea:

```
for(int b = 0; b < __v ; ++b)
    if(adj[i][b])
        dp[i][j][e] += dp[b][j][e - 1];
```

The pseudocode is as follows:

```
for(int e = 0; e <= k; ++ e)
{
    for(int i = 0;i < __v; ++ i)
    {
        for(int j = 0;j < __v; ++ j)
        {
            // initialize
            dp[i][j][e] = 0;

            // base cases
            if(e == 0 && i == j)
                dp[i][j][e] = 1;
            if(e == 1 && adj[i][j])
                dp[i][j][e] = 1;

            // go to adjacent edges only when number of
edges is more than 1
            if(e>1)
            {
                for(int b = 0; b < __v ; ++ b)
                {
                    if(adj[i][b])
                    {
                        dp[i][j][e] += dp[b][j][e - 1];
                    }
                }
            }
        }
    }
}
// number of paths from u to v with k edges
return dp[u][v][k];
```

If you observe carefully, the time complexity to calculate dp[u][v][k] is $O(V^3 * K)$. We have improved this significantly as we have gone from an exponential time complexity to a polynomial time complexity.

Divide and Conquer Approach

We can optimize this further by using a **divide and conquer approach**.

We can use divide and conquer approach to solve this problem in $O(V^3\log_2 k)$ **time**, to this we use the fact that the number of paths of length k from u to v is the [u][v]th entry in the matrix $(adj[V][V])^k$.
The kth power of a graph G is a graph with the same set of vertices as G and an edge between two vertices if and only if there is a path of length at most k between them. Since a path of length two between vertices u and v exists for every vertex w such that {u,w} and {w,v} are edges in G, the square of the adjacency matrix of G counts the number of such paths. Similarly, the [u][v]th element of the kth power of the adjacency matrix of G gives the number of paths of length k between vertices u and v.

To understand why this holds true, follow along. In the first case of adjacency matrix, it is natural that it holds true as a path of length 1 is one edge which is that the two vertices are directly connected.

When we raised the adjacency matrix to the power of 2, for a given index, we compute the multiplication of that particular row with the column that passes through the index. Let the index be (x, y). In this case, the row denotes how vertex x is connected to other vertices. The column denotes how other vertices are connected to vertex y.

When we are multiplying this, we are computing the combination of elements of a row with elements of the column. In our case, a row represents how a vertex is linked to other vertices and the column represents how other vertices are linked with the current vertex. By multiplying, we are incrementally increasing the length of path.

This is an important concept. Think about this deeply.

At this point, if we simply perform multiplication and get the adjacency matrix raised to the power of K, we will get the same time complexity. To improve it, we need to optimize this step which can be done using the idea that raising to the power of 2 eliminates several multiplications.

For example, instead of computing power of 5, we can compute 2 times power of 2 followed by a multiplication which results in the same answer.

To find $(adj[V][V])^k$, we use the divide and conquer approach of finding power(x, y) in $O(\log_2 y)$ time that is this algorithm is an application of **fast matrix exponentiation**.

Fast matrix exponentiation is based on the same principle we explained and is applicable on numeric data other than matrix as well.

The idea is:

$$A^N = (A^{N/2})^2 \text{ if N is even}$$

$$A^N = (A^{(N-1)/2})^2 * A \text{ if N is odd}$$

This is computed recursively that is same rules apply to $A^{N/2}$ as to A^N. This reduces the number of multiplications from N to logN.

The pseudocode of this approach is as follows:

```
// Function to compute adjacency_matrix raise to power k.
power(adjacency_matrix, u, v, k)
{
    __v = adj.size();
    result[][];

    for(int i = 0; i < __v; ++i)
        result [i][i] = 1;

    while (k > 0)
    {
        if (k % 2 == 1)
```

```
                  result = multiply(result,
adjacency_matrix);
            adjacency_matrix = multiply(adjacency_matrix,
adjacency_matrix);
            k /= 2;
    }
    // number of paths from u to v with k edges
    return result [u][v];
}
```

Following is the complexity summary of the approaches we have explored:

Time Complexity

- Brute Force approach takes **O(2^V x V) time**
- Structured Brute force approach takes **O(V^k) time**.
- DP approach takes **O(V^3k) time**.
- Divide and Conquer approach takes **O($V^3\log_2 k$) time**.

Space Complexity

- Brute Force approach takes **O(2^V)** space as we need to store all generated paths. We can avoid storing paths and in this case, the space complexity will be **O(V)** for the temporary path.
- Structured Brute force approach takes **O(V^2)** auxiliary space and **O(V^k)** stack space.
- DP approach takes **O(V^2k)** auxiliary space.

- Divide and conquer takes $O(V^2)$ auxiliary space.

Hence, we can see that our final divide and conquer approach works better than the Dynamic Programming approach both in terms of time and space complexity.

- Graph problems at OpenGenus: iq.opengenus.org/tag/graph-algorithm/
- Dynamic Programming problems at OpenGenus: iq.opengenus.org/tag/dynamic-programming/
- Divide and Conquer problems at OpenGenus: iq.opengenus.org/tag/divide-and-conquer/

We just solved a problem that is in the intersection of Graph Theory and Dynamic Programming. Enjoy.

With this, we have come to the end of our short book to bring you into the mindset of solving Graph Algorithms problems for the day before your Coding Interview.

With the ideas we have explored, we can solve a wide range of problems. Consider the problem of **finding the shortest path between all vertices in a Graph**.

We can solve this using the ideas from our first problem to formulate a working Brute Force approach. It will be exponential in time complexity $O(2^V \times V^3)$.

Based on the Dynamic Programming approach we have taken in our third problem, we can solve this in $O(V^3)$ time. This is known as Floyd Warshall Algorithm (Read more: Floyd Warshall Algorithm).

This specific problem can be solved more efficiently for specific sparse graphs (with less edges) using an algorithm known as Johnson's Algorithm. It uses several standard algorithms internally (Read more: iq.opengenus.org/johnson-algorithm/).

Hence, think about the problems we have explored deeply and implement it in a Programming Language you are comfortable with. You will be able to solve every Graph based problem.

iq.opengenus.org

 discuss.opengenus.org

 team@opengenus.org

 amazon.opengenus.org

 linkedIn.opengenus.org

 github.opengenus.org

 twitter.opengenus.org

 facebook.opengenus.org

 instagram.opengenus.org

Feel free to get in touch with us and enjoy learning and solving computational problems.